Rock Painting for
KIDS!

LET'S ROCK!

Updated Edition

LINDA KRANZ

Photography by Klaus Kranz

muddy boots
CALGARY PUBLIC LIBRARY
no jump in puddles
Guilford, Connecticut
JUN   2018

Published by Muddy Boots
An imprint of Globe Pequot
MuddyBootsBooks.com

Distributed by NATIONAL BOOK NETWORK

Copyright © 2017 Linda Kranz
Illustrations © 2017 Linda Kranz
Photography by Klaus Kranz
Design by Maria Kauffman
Edited by Theresa Howell

British Library Cataloguing-in-Publication Information available
Library of Congress Cataloging-in-Publication Data available

ISBN 978-1-63076-294-0 (paperback)
ISBN 978-1-63076-295-7 (e-book)

Printed in China

FOR MR. DUREN,
my art teacher at Bitburg American High School, Bitburg, Germany. Thank you for your encouragement. You made a difference!

AND FOR EVERY ARTIST:
Never let anyone discourage you from expressing your creative side. Share your talents with others. With art you always leave something of yourself behind.

TABLE OF CONTENTS

INTRODUCTION

PAINTING is like fishing. What? Ok, let me explain. My husband Klaus says when he is fly fishing, standing in a clear mountain stream, watching the current, and noticing certain movements in the water, he's so focused he actually loses track of time. That's how I feel when I'm painting at my art table. I'm noticing colors, the lines. I'm watching an idea I had come to life. I'm completely lost in the moment. When you are doing something you enjoy, time flies. That's why I say painting is like fishing.

I began painting in high school. I took all of the required classes, but the one class I really looked forward to every day was art. Our art classes only went up to the eleventh grade, so when I was a senior, my art

This is one of my very first painted rocks. The rock surface was smooth and it had a small flat area that allowed the design to fit into it. I didn't paint a base coat on the entire rock. I left it natural. You can look for rocks to paint on, which you can leave the background natural as well.

teacher convinced the school staff that he had a handful of students who "needed" to continue on in art. Finally, an advanced art class was offered. Our teacher was there to guide us, yet he let us be creative. That's where my love for art began. I remember painting a huge mural near the school office. It was quite an undertaking, but it was worth it because I received many compliments from my classmates, which made my spirits soar!

After high school our family moved to Arizona. Growing up, we had only lived on the East Coast and in Germany so we had a lot of exploring to do. While out hiking one day, I happened on a rock that offered a nice flat surface I could paint on. I was hooked. I began noticing rocks, and rocks became my canvas.

While enjoying the outdoors, not only did I notice rocks I could paint on, I began to notice rocks patterns. Banded rocks. Rocks with vivid colors. Translucent rocks. Rocks that took on a particular shape. One

I have beautiful natural rocks in bowls or jars around our house. They are nature's art and should be enjoyed.

year, while on vacation in Colorado, I was looking for postcards to send to family and friends and I noticed a postcard that had a photograph of several heart-shaped rocks. I thought to myself, wouldn't that be something to find a heart-shaped rock? I started looking, and to my delight I began to find heart-shaped rocks. With a trained eye and just the right concentration, you'll find heart rocks, too!

In this book, you will find the rock-painting techniques I've developed over time and many different design ideas. Patterns for

This is the back of a rock I painted for my husband when we were first married. On the front, there is a colorful design. This was my very first attempt at painting on rocks. All these years later, it still looks great!

Walking along the banks of a small stream, our son spotted this buffalo-shaped rock. Some rocks just instantly catch your eye; others are camouflaged and take more concentration to see.

most of the designs can be found in the back. This book is designed to inspire you as you grow as an artist. There's something for you to create at every stage: simple, middle of the road, and very detailed. No matter what, my hope is that this book will remain on your bookshelf for years and you will refer back to it time and time again.

Be patient, have fun, and enjoy!

LINDA KRANZ

HELPFUL HINTS

Just for you! Wherever you see Helpful Hints as you read through Let's Rock!, there will be additional fun things for you to try and helpful hints that will make your rocks REALLY ROCK!

I am the author and illustrator of many books in which the illustrations are made up entirely of my own painted rocks! Here are Mama, Papa, and Adri from Only One You.

"Every child is an artist—
the problem is how to remain
an artist once you grow up."

–PABLO PICASSO

GETTING STARTED

LET'S TALK ROCKS

THE BEST ROCKS

Smooth, flat rocks work best. It's better if they are non-porous. Otherwise, the paint will soak in and you'll end up painting lots of coats. That takes extra time and extra paint. Bumpy rocks add interesting details, but again, it's better if they are non-porous.

You can paint on rocks of any size. If you see a pattern in this book that you would like to paint and your rock is larger than the pattern in the book, you can increase the size of the pattern on a copy machine so that it fits the rock that you have found.

FIRST you'll need to find your rocks. That's the fun part! You can find them in ordinary places like on the playground, in your backyard or garden, at friends' houses, in riverbeds, or if all else fails, at landscape or garden supply stores. Rocks are everywhere! Suggest that your family go on a rock-finding outing some weekend. Once relatives and friends hear that you paint rocks, they will find rocks for you. Guaranteed! Friends are always sending me rocks that I can paint.

The rock shown on the left has a bumpy, porous surface, and the rock above has a smooth surface. Either one will work for painting the design you choose, but porous rocks will need extra base coats to cover the rock well.

HELPFUL HINTS

Find your rocks in the spring, summer, or fall. Then when winter sets in and your time outdoors is limited or the landscape is buried in snow, all you have to do is reach into your basket of clean rocks and you are ready to paint. Make some art! Cozy and warm inside.

This bundle of rocks offers a large selection of shapes and sizes. If you don't have time to set off on a hike to find rocks, check out a few stores near where you live.

INSPIRATION

Inspiration can be found anywhere—in the clouds, on a sidewalk, or in a field of flowers. Artists are always on the lookout for ideas that will inspire them to create. Just use your imagination!

Try looking for rocks that resemble things, such as animals or food or a heart. Sometimes the shape of a rock will inspire you to paint something that the rock reminds you of. You can start a collection. One thing is for sure, once you start collecting them, you will never look at rocks the same way again. Now that you are a painter of rocks, you will always be searching for that perfect rock to paint.

As an artist I'm always noticing details, shapes, patterns, and colors when I'm out and about. I have plain paper in my handbag. If something catches my attention, I sketch it out. Later I will put the drawing on a shelf next to my art table. I never know when that idea will come in handy. You would be surprised how many times I have referred back to those sketches.

One afternoon as I glanced up at the sky, I saw a shape in the clouds that looked like a pterodactyl. I quickly took a picture. Later I sketched out the design and then I painted the shape on a rock.

Sometimes you will find rocks in nature that remind you of something. I found the rock on the left while hiking. Do you see the giraffe in the outline? I showed it to several people and they couldn't see it. When I painted the rock below and held it next to the natural rock, they smiled and said, "Oh, now I see it!"

Walking in our neighborhood park one morning, I happened to glance down at the sidewalk. A penguin. Inspiration is all around us.

11

STUFF YOU WILL NEED

PAINT

Acrylic paint works best for painting rocks—it dries fast, covers well, and if you make a mistake, you can just cover it up with more paint! You can buy a few basic colors and mix your own or buy a large variety of colors.

These days the colors are so versatile and there is such a wide variety to choose from, I would recommend buying colors you can use right out of the tube or container: orange for a pumpkin, green for a frog, blue for the sky, white for a moon, or red for a heart. Then if you want to mix the colors to have lighter or darker shades, you could do that too.

It's important to buy white paint to be used as the base coat on your rocks. White paint comes in handy for touch-ups as well.

BRUSHES

You can buy a few brushes to start out with, and then, over time, add to your collection. Buy a variety of different sizes. If you take care of your brushes, they will last you a long, long time.

PAINT TRAY & CONTAINERS

You can buy a small paint tray. There are several sizes to choose from at craft or art supply stores. Some artists use a paper plate to put their paint on or mix their paint colors. An egg carton, an old ice cube tray, or an empty butter dish can also be used in a pinch. Whatever you use, it must be very clean, dry, and free of oil residues, which can interfere with your acrylic paints.

Keep clean water on your art table in a washed-out yogurt cup for washing out your brushes after you change paint colors.

PAPER

You'll need paper for covering your work surface and paper to place under your rock while you paint. Plain white or brown paper, like a cut-open grocery sack, is best.

HELPFUL HINTS

If you need to mix a color, make sure you mix enough so that you'll have some left over for touch-ups. It will be almost impossible to mix that exact color again. Mixed paints, stored in tiny cups with lids, will last for several days. If you use paint colors directly from the tube, touch-ups will be a breeze.

"Imagination is more important than knowledge. Knowledge is limited. Imagination encircles the world."

—ALBERT EINSTEIN

NOW LET'S
PAINT

PREPARING YOUR ROCK

YOU will need a good base coat on the bottom and the top of your rock. The base coat is important because it helps the other colors adhere better to the rock. Plus, your finished painting will be much brighter with a base coat underneath the colorful paint.

On the top of your rock, a thick base coat will give you a nice surface on which to trace your pattern and paint your design. If you only have a light layer of paint on the top, the pencil will be very faint. You will be guessing and squinting trying to paint inside the lines of your pattern. The base coat on the bottom of your rock doesn't have to be as thick, but it's still important. As you paint more rocks, you will come to know just how much base coat you need.

STEPS

1. Rinse the rock well in warm water. Pat dry with paper towels and allow to air dry completely.

2. Lay the rock on a flat surface. Choose which side will be the "bottom" or underside of the rock, according to which side lays flat best. You will paint your design on the "top" of the rock. For example, the rock on the left in the picture would wobble if you touched it. If you turn that rock over and place the flat side down like the rock on the right, you'll find you have a much more stable surface on which to paint.

Notice the rock on the far left. The colors seem faded or muted. The yellow-orange paint was applied directly onto the natural rock. The first strip has one coat. The middle strip has two coats. The far-right strip has three coats. Now look at the rock that has the white base coat applied first. It's a remarkable difference, don't you agree? Base-coating your rock first makes your beautiful art work vibrant!!!

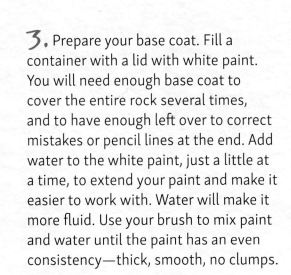

3. Prepare your base coat. Fill a container with a lid with white paint. You will need enough base coat to cover the entire rock several times, and to have enough left over to correct mistakes or pencil lines at the end. Add water to the white paint, just a little at a time, to extend your paint and make it easier to work with. Water will make it more fluid. Use your brush to mix paint and water until the paint has an even consistency—thick, smooth, no clumps.

4. Cover your work area with paper. Paint the bottom of your rock with base coat. Smooth out any bubbles or uneven paint by brushing over the rock in one direction. Allow to air dry. Repeat this step several times, allowing paint to air dry between each coat. The layers of base coat do not have to be very thick at all, but you will need multiple layers.

5. When the bottom of the rock is completely dry, turn the rock over and base coat the top of the rock with several coats. The top of your rock needs a thicker base coat cover than the bottom. While the rock is drying between coats, wash your brush out well with water (soap is not necessary) and squeeze out excess water. This will prevent your paint from clumping when you paint again.

17

PAINTING YOUR DESIGN

3. Put the cutout, pencil-traced side down, on the rock. Now trace the lines of your design onto the rock. Don't worry about erasing any extra pencil marks or smears. You can always touch up with your white base coat. Wait for the white paint to dry.

STEPS

1. Choose the design you wish to paint on your rock. You could pick a design from the book or draw your own. If you choose to draw your own design, lay your rock on plain paper and draw around the rock to get the shape and size. Then draw your design inside the rock outline.

4. Once the design has been traced, look at your original pattern and lightly draw in the design that is missing on your rock.

2. Cut out your design. Go to a window, turn the pattern to touch the glass, and carefully trace the outline of your pattern on the back side of the cutout.

5. Paint your design with your chosen color and allow to air dry completely.

6. Paint the background color on the top and sides of your rock. You may need to apply more than one coat of paint to your design and background. Remember to let your rock dry between coats.

FINISHING TOUCHES

1. When your rock is completely dry, you may wish to outline your design with black paint or another color paint. Or you can use a fine point permanent pen.

2. When the top of your rock is completely dry, it's time to clean up any paint lines or smudges on the back or sides of your rock. Now use your original colors to clean up any uneven paint lines or smudges. (This is where using the colors right out of the tube comes in handy. It makes touch-ups a snap!)

3. Allow your finished rock to air dry completely, and then give it to someone you love, or keep it for yourself!

HELPFUL HINTS

Carry the main background color—in this case sky blue—onto the backside of your rock. You can turn your rock over and paint the back side when the top of your rock is completely finished and dry. It makes for a clean finished-looking rock.

WRITING ON ROCKS

2. Go to a window and trace on top of each letter in your word. Cut off the top and bottom of the traced pattern. Trim both of the pattern sides a bit, leaving room so your fingers can hold onto the pattern as you position the pattern with the word onto your rock just where you want it.

STEPS

1. Trace around your natural rock on a piece of lined notebook paper. What do you want to write on your rock? Write your word on the lined paper, making sure it's centered and neatly written. Practice a few times if you would like.

3. Base coat your rock. Once the base coat is dry you can paint your rock a color of your choice.

4. Place your pattern onto your painted rock with the pencil-traced side facing down. When you have your pattern right where it looks best, hold it very steady, and with a ball point pen, very slowly trace your letters, applying good pressure.

You can also print out a word or words from your computer and size it to fit your rock, leaving room to hold onto the pattern.

If you trace lightly you won't be able to see the words. Do not lift the pattern; just keep on task. Moving the pattern will shift the place you are, so carefully hold the pattern in place. Don't rush. Slow and easy. It may take a few times to master this skill. Soon you will be a pro!

5. Now that your words are on the rock you can paint them with a fine brush or use a permanent marker. If you have some stray pencil or paint marks, touch them up with the color of paint you painted your rock.

For thicker letters, fill in the letters with white paint. When the white paint has dried, paint over the white with a color of your choice. Outline the letters using permanent marker or black paint.

Ready · Visualize · Fun · YES! · Smile · Calm · Kindness · Focus · Notice · Never give up · I can do this! · Try · Joy · Gratitude · Read · Practice · Good choices · Wow! · Patience · Love · I'm me

Inspiration to go. Before you head out the door to greet your day, reach into your plate of words and choose a rock that will be meaningful for you to carry with you in a zippered pouch in your backpack or in your pocket. It's a gentle reminder that stays with you. When you put that rock back on your plate, stop and think about how the rock nudged you to think about that word all day. Tomorrow you may want to choose another word or you might want to carry the same word with you all week. It's up to you.

"When you can do the common things of life in an uncommon way, you will command the attention of the world."

—GEORGE WASHINGTON CARVER

Nature

Stay Strong!

DESIGN
IDEAS

A FLOWER FOR YOU

HOW can you see a design in a rock? Use your imagination! If a rock catches my eye, I pick it up and study the size and shape. I think about the many possibilities for painting a design on that particular rock. I love to paint flowers on rocks to give to friends or loved ones on special occasions. Unlike store-bought flowers or flowers from the garden, a flower rock will always stay "fresh." Why not paint a flower rock for someone special? Or maybe a whole bouquet of colorful painted rock flowers?

STEPS

1. Paint the base coat and draw your design on the rock. Then paint your flower any color you wish. Allow the paint to dry.

2. Paint the leaves. Allow the paint to dry.

3. Choose the background color. Paint around the leaves and the flower. When your rock is completely dry, you may wish to outline your design and add more details with paint or pen.

HELPFUL HINTS

Throughout the book you will see rocks that are smaller than other rocks. I call these "pocket rocks." They fit nicely in your pocket. You could paint one for yourself or a friend as a reminder of something. You could paint a pattern on the front. A star. A cloud. A sun. A rainbow. And on the back you could paint or write a message in your tiniest handwriting: Smile. Try. Laugh. Dream. Be Happy. Just be sure that if you carry it in your pocket, you take it out before laundry day!

AWESOME ANIMALS

ANIMALS are everywhere. They share our houses with us. They live in our backyards and in our towns and cities. There are many different types of animals we can paint on rocks. Ideas are all around us. You could paint a bird that lands on a branch outside your window. Or you could paint an animal you remember seeing while you were on vacation. Look around for ideas.

HELPFUL HINTS

Use a paper napkin to take excess paint off your brush. When you are painting, you don't want a bubble of paint on your brush. If a big drop of paint covers more than you had planned, you will have to let that area dry and repaint it. That's frustrating. I always keep a napkin next to my paint tray—it comes in handy!

Some rocks will remind you of an animal just by their shape. This rock was in the shape of a cat's head when I found it. Even the ears were in the perfect spot! This duck looks so much like a duck, it could almost quack!

STEPS

1. Paint the base coat and draw the rabbit design on your rock.

2. Pick the color you want to use for your rabbit. Paint the body of the rabbit. Allow the paint to dry. Paint the grass. Paint the sky.

3. Paint the rabbit's face. Allow the paint to dry. Paint the eyes. Allow the paint to dry. When your rock is completely dry, use paint or pen to outline your rabbit and fill in the details on the body, face, eyes, ears, and paws.

MORE AMAZING ANIMALS

HERE are lots of ideas for painting different animals. Don't forget—the patterns for these rocks are in the back of the book! Have fun and use your imagination.

Hold a rock in your hand for a while when you find it. Turn it over a few times. Use your imagination. What do you see? Some animals fit perfectly on round rocks. Sometimes you might be able to find other rocks that look just like the shape of an animal.

How about a trip to the zoo for more ideas to paint? You can take a picture of your favorite animals or bring a pad and pencil along and draw the animals that you want to paint.

Create a prehistoric scene with different landscapes and dinosaurs. You could even paint a pterodactyl flying in the sky overhead.

HELPFUL HINTS

What should you paint first? That's up to you. I paint the main design, the background, and then the black outline.

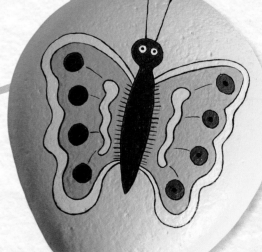

You can find different sized rocks and paint a family of animals like these crocodiles.

LOVELY HEARTS

ABOVE everything else, love! Have you ever searched for a heart rock? They are everywhere just waiting for someone to find them. I have found heart rocks in the country and in the city. You just have to train your eyes to see them. If you can't find a rock shaped like a heart, look for a rock with a nice, smooth surface on which to paint a heart. Heart rocks are wonderful to give for Valentine's Day or any time you just want to say, "I love you."

Paint a heart on a rock and send the rock to someone special. Tuck a note in the package that says, "When you look at this painted heart rock, always remember, *I love you!*" Giving a rock of love is a reminder that your love is always and forever.

SUPER SPORTY

Go TEAM!

A ball is a perfect subject to paint for someone you know who has a favorite sport. You can search for a rock that is round. If you can't find one that's round, don't worry. Just find a rock with a flat surface and paint the shape of the ball on the rock. You could paint a ball to give to someone for winning a big game or tournament. Or you could paint one for yourself to remember a special achievement in a game. Whether the rock is for a friend or for yourself, paint or write the date of the game on the back of the rock so it will never be forgotten.

Notice the two football shapes on this page. Both look like a football, but they are each on different shaped rocks. One football has a blue background so it looks like it's flying through the air for a touchdown. The other football takes on the entire shape of the rock. You could also paint a ball with a green background so it looks like it's resting in a field of grass. There are lots of options.

Tee time? You can paint rocks to have a three-dimensional look. Notice the white area painted in between the gray circles and ovals on this golf ball. Paint the area. Let it dry. Paint the area again. Let it dry. As each coat dries and you add a new layer of white paint, slowly the white paint builds up, giving the rock a three-dimensional look. Continue this process for as many as eight coats. It's a long process, but I think you will like the unique look. Also look at the bagel on the Let's Eat! pages. I built up the paint on that rock as well.

A hockey puck sliding across the ice!

You could paint a beach ball to remind a friend or a loved one about a summer vacation you took together.

HELPFUL HINTS

I like to keep my paints in a plastic box with a lid. That way they are all in one place. And if you have little brothers or sisters who are curious, they won't be able to get into them as easily. I write down all the colors I have in my plastic paint box. Then when I go to the craft store, I bring the list along so I don't buy duplicate colors. Remember to add any new colors you buy to your list.

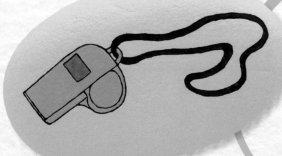

A whistle rock can make a great gift for your favorite coach.

PRETTY PLACES

WE all have our favorite places that we like to visit or dream about. For some it's the big city. Cities have their own beauty. Day or night. Others may prefer a quiet field in a forest to set up camp for a few days. Some people dream about a secluded island retreat. The desert? The mountains? Where do your dreams take you?

Here's an idea: Perhaps you live in Arizona and your grandparents who live on the East Coast visited you and your family over spring break. They were able to explore where you live, and they talked about how beautiful the desert was. Why not paint them a rock with a desert scene on it and send them a little package with your painted rock to remind them of the special vacation you spent together? I think they would love it.

STEPS

1. Paint the base coat and draw your design on the rock. Start painting the light green trees.

2. Paint the dark green trees. Paint the low bushes. Paint the sky. Paint the lake.

3. Paint the clouds. Outline the details with black paint or permanent pen.

LET'S EAT!

SOMETIMES when you look around you get all kinds of great ideas for painting on rocks. What about painting some of your favorite foods? A juicy cheeseburger? A veggie burger? A hot dog? A taco with avocado? How about a slice of watermelon to help you cool off on a hot summer day? Chocolate chip cookies are always a treat. Or maybe you prefer a gingerbread cookie? How about a scrambled egg bagel sandwich? Or pancakes and a tasty slice of orange? Think of some other foods that you could paint.

Warning: Looking at this page might make you hungry. But then who wants to eat a rock, right?

Is someone you know celebrating a birthday? Paint them a birthday cupcake with a candle so they can make a wish. Do they like chocolate or vanilla?

Notice the natural rock on the left of the painted hot dog. When you are out searching for interesting rocks, look for this shape and you can paint your own hot dog or chili dog.

"Pizza tastes good any day of the week," a friend once told me.

HELPFUL HINTS

If you have been painting for a long time, find a stopping point. Get up. Stretch. Rest your eyes. When you come back to your rock, study the design. Look at the colors. Stepping away and coming back gives you a whole new perspective. If you don't like how the colors look, you can paint over the colors you don't like. That's the nice thing about acrylic paints— they are very easy to work with.

THINGS THAT GO

THERE are so many different ways to get from here to there. By car, by truck, by bike—what is your favorite way to get around? This train is about the head into the tunnel. Notice the last train car. When the train comes out the other side, the last car will be carrying anything you want. What would you put in your last train car? Art supplies? Your favorite books? Musical instruments? Sketch out your ideas and start painting!

Go Fish

I LOVE painting fish rocks—always smiling, happy, carefree, each with a different unique pattern. Years ago, I found a rock that sat flat and offered a space that allowed me to create a mini aquarium. The best part? You never have to change the water! Just dust it from time to time.

STEPS

1. Paint some flowing grasses on the bottom of the rock.

2. Paint a fish or two. Glue on the fish on top of the grasses.

3. Glue on a few colorful shells. Now the aquarium is ready to display!

STORY ROCKS

TELL A STORY!

STORIES fill our lives from the time we are young. are read stories. Our parents, grandparents, relatives, and friends share personal stories from their lives: happy times, times they were surprised, times that made them stop and think and question where do I go from here? As a storyteller you weave a story and hopefully the listeners will be spellbound by your retelling of what it was like when . . .

MAP

MAP

Mountain Trail

Valley Trail

FINDING INSPIRATION

Create a group of rocks. You can also choose designs from any of the rocks you see on the pages in this book. Pick up a paint brush and create your own unique rocks. When you have assembled a good variety, sit with those rocks all around you and think about how you can bring to a story to life, real or imagined. Next pick up your pen and start writing! Keep creating new stories and fine-tuning the stories that you have written. You will notice your descriptions over time will become more interesting. Your sentences will be tighter. Your stories will be so interesting to read and share.

SHARING STORIES

You can even turn your story rocks into a game! Bring your rocks with you and create a story with a friend. Each storyteller can pull out one rock at a time and add on to the story based on the picture on the rock he or she pulls. It's fun to see what twists and turns the story will take! You can even write down your "interwoven friend story" as a memory to look back on. Tuck it away. I'll bet it will be something special to share and read again several months later!

43

ROCKIN' IDEAS

SHARE A SMILE

These happy faces would make a welcome addition to a classroom to encourage students who might be struggling with a task. Having a colorful smile on their desk is a great way to boost their confidence. And when a student has worked very hard to achieve a particular goal, they could have a satisfied smile sitting on their desk. *I did it!*

At day's end, the smiles are returned back to the bowl or basket, resting up for the next student's desk.

Teachers could make up the smiles over the summer and have them ready for the start of the school year. Maybe a few parents could get together and create the smiles together. One thing's for sure: they will brighten a student's day!

TIC-TAC-TOE

Here is a colorful way to play the game of tic-tac-toe. Instead of Xs and Os, it's cats vs. dogs! Who do you think will win? What are some other design ideas you could use for the game pieces?

CAIRNS

They mark trails for us so we can find our way back to our cars when we are out hiking. Visually they are beautiful to look at. Often they make us stop and wonder, "How did someone stack those rocks so neatly? Why aren't they falling over?" You could make a cairn created from natural rocks or a cairn of painted rocks. Stacking rocks requires a lot of patience, an attribute we could all benefit from, right? So stack away!

MAGNETS

To turn your painted rocks into magnets, all you need is a roll of small round magnets and some glue! Display your magnets on the fridge to hold appointment reminders and your very own art. Give a few magnets to family members or your teacher. Everyone can use a handful of magnets.

Book club meets in library after school

Soccer Practice today at 4:00.

LOVE love love love

HAPPY happy HAPPY

TODAY IS awesome

Make Art!

PAPERWEIGHTS

Find a rock that has a great surface to paint a design on and a flat bottom. Choose a pattern that will catch your eye. Glue a piece of felt to the bottom of your painted rock. Now you've created a paperweight that will capture your attention and keep those reminders or special papers organized and easy to find.

46

JEWELRY

Natural rocks make beautiful necklaces and painted rocks that you have created offer a way to show your family and friends your artistic talents. All you need to turn your favorite rocks into jewelry are a necklace mount, a cord, and some glue!

First, choose a rock that has a nice shape that will look great hanging on your necklace. After you have created your design, glue the mount (seen above) to the back of your rock. A variety of mounts and cording can be found at your local craft shop. Now you have a unique piece of jewelry!

GIFT ROCKS

Gifts come in all shapes and sizes. It is wonderful to give someone a gift you have created that is one-of-a-kind. I guarantee your special someone will thank you for your present!

Inside this present I put a colorful rainbow, the song of a bird, a smile, a great big hug, and the sound of my laugh.

Good choices

Imagine

Dream

NOW THE PATTERNS

"I dream my painting, and then I paint my dream."

—VINCENT VAN GOGH

THESE next few pages are filled with lots of patterns for you to use. Cut the patterns right out of the book or use tracing paper to trace over the designs you want to use. Transfer paper is also something you could use. If you cut out the patterns, store them in an envelope and slide it into this book. That way, all your patterns will be in one place in case you want to reuse them.

What if you find a rock that is a different size from a pattern you want to use? Just ask a grown-up to make you a larger or smaller copy using a copy machine so the pattern will fit nicely onto your rock. If you would like the design on a pattern to face the opposite direction, no problem. Instead of tracing the outline of your pattern on the backside, make your pencil-tracing directly on the pattern's lines. Turn the pattern to touch your base-coated rock and the pattern is now facing the opposite direction.

This is a book of ideas. We all want to be creative. Once you feel comfortable, add your own touch to the rock designs in this book, or create your own new designs. You are the artist! Have fun!

I would love to hear from you. You can visit my website at lindakranz.com.

Notice the rocks on the right. When you choose your rock, size doesn't matter. You can resize your pattern to fit any size rock.

48

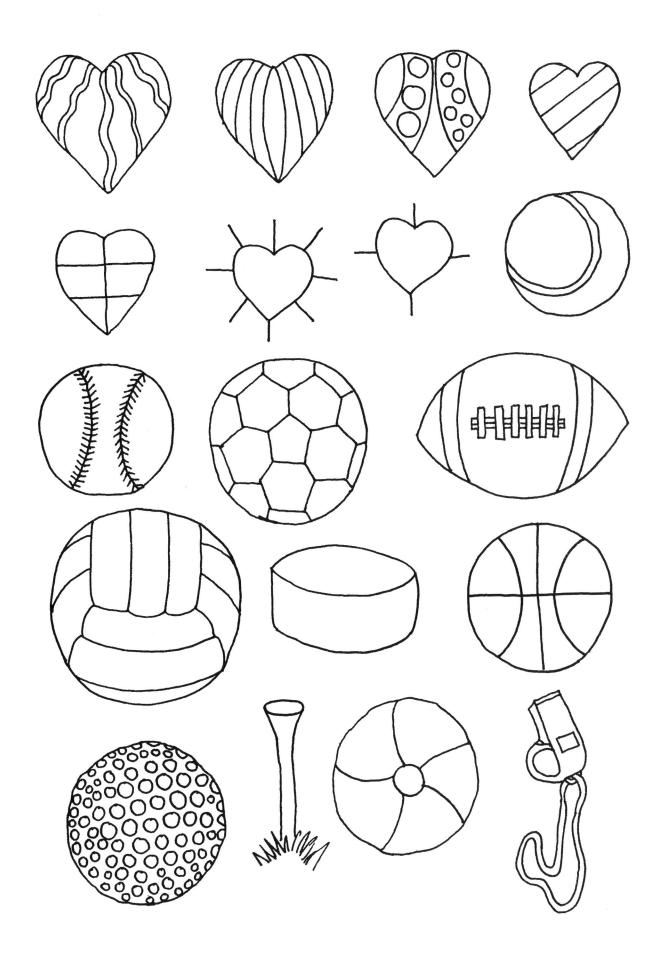

School